AF193928

Socialist Renewal

The first series of Socialist Renewal publications grew out of the discussions around Labour's abandonment of Clause Four, in 1995. A general invitation was issued to socialist authors to write for us. A dozen pamphlets and half a dozen books followed. They probed the transport crisis in Britain, common ownership, pensions and national insurance, the rights of the unemployed, as well as the threat to peace posed by Nato's expansion. Many of these early criticisms of New Labour in opposition have proved only too well-founded by the experience of New Labour in government.

Because of this adverse experience of New Labour , a number of people asked us to launch a second series of Socialist Renewal titles. We consulted about this, and received a very encouraging response. Our new invitation to write provoked a number of exciting proposals which will help to clarify the arguments which are developing on the Left. You will find a list of the first titles in the new series at the end of this pamphlet. More information is available on our web site (www.spokesmanbooks.com).

Further titles in the pipeline will challenge the privatisation of air traffic control and make the case for returning the railways to public ownership; address the crisis in education with the privatisation of local education authorities and business influence on the curriculum; expose the ruination of much of higher education and set out an alternative vision for universities and colleges; and examine the continuing crisis in the health service. We shall also be publishing an analysis of New Labour's economic policy, and initiating a discussion of their foreign and security policies.

A subscription to Socialist Renewal costs £15 for 10 titles, payable to 'Bertrand Russell House', Russell House, Bulwell Lane, Nottingham NG6 0BT.

PUBLIC SERVICES
or
CORPORATE WELFARE

Rethinking the Nation State
in the Global Economy
by Dexter Whitfield

**An essential, insightful and thought-provoking
NEW book which:**

- provides a radical analysis of modernisation including partnerships, private finance and Best Value;

- analyses how the state facilitates globalisation by promoting private finance and the marketisation of public services;

- exposes how the Third Way masks the continuity of neo-liberalism;

- demonstrates how the World Trade Organisation is committed to privatising public services and welfare states;

- charts the emergence of a Corporate-Welfare Complex;

- promotes a revitalised role for the state in a new system of global governance, stressing the importance of sustaining and improving the welfare state;

- advocates a dynamic new model of public service management placing priority on innovation, equality and investment as an alternative to the reinvention and performance management models.

Published by Pluto Press (www.plutobooks.com)
Paperback: ISBN 0 7453 0856 2   Price £16.99.
Hardback: ISBN 0 7453 0855 4   Price £50.00

Public Services or Private Profit?

By Dexter Whitfield

Introduction

Politicians and academics examine the causes of alienation, disillusionment and disconnectedness from the political process but they fail to understand that many people feel a deep sense of policy betrayal. They are not taken in by tokenistic focus groups or service charters to patch over the continued growth of unelected, unaccountable quasi-public bodies and the centralisation of decision-making. People also object to the enforced use of private capital and cosying up to big business allegedly in order to improve local facilities. Thatcherism succeeded in creating a more selfish, individualistic 'me' society, and instead of promoting a new social and collective ideology, Labour's Third Way 'new individualism' appears to blame 'failing' schools, under-performing services, single mothers and the unemployed.

Labour's modernisation programme has seven fault lines. The first extends from the ideology of 'what matters is what works'. This neutrality on who provides services results in a failure to provide leadership in promoting public management. The second fault line extends through performance management with the emphasis on benchmarking, efficiency, outcomes, audit and inspection at the expense of other values and the process of provision. The third fault line is competition which is embedded in the modernisation programme, thus extending marketisation and privatisation.

Public Private Partnership/Private Finance Initiative projects are the fourth fault line, encompassing the welfare infrastructure. These are justified solely on financial grounds and the private sector's claims of efficiency, expertise and value for money. The fifth fault line runs through the opposing policies of joined-up government and the transfer of core services to quangos, together with the proliferation of zones, contracts and initiatives. The aims of democratic renewal are weakened by more secretive cabinet government, consumerism and lack of capacity building to replace the development resources stripped from communities over the last two decades. This makes involvement, let alone empowerment, improbable. This is the sixth fault line. Finally, although local government has new powers for community planning and social, economic and environmental well-being, the combination of the fault lines reduces the capacity of public bodies to use these powers effectively.

This pamphlet is based on my book *Public Services or Corporate Welfare: Rethinking the Nation State in the Global Economy* (Pluto Press, 2001).

I
'Modernising' the State

Between 1979 and 1997, the British state was subject to radical restructuring and privatisation on a scale unparalleled among major industrialised economies. Restructuring in New Zealand went further and deeper but, as a relatively small economy, was not as influential as Thatcherism. Second, since 1997 the Labour government has led the way in promoting the Third Way as an alternative to neo-liberalism. It has led the world in private finance and partnerships for renewal of the welfare state social infrastructure as well as the transport and communications infrastructure. It is also continuing the restructuring of the welfare state, largely copying US reforms. This has serious implications for other European countries.

Criticism of Nationalisation

By the early 1970s public services in Britain, particularly the nationalised industries, required reform which, following a period of rapid post-war growth and investment, was inevitable. Democratic accountability was weak, often characterised by poor management in bureaucratic, hierarchical and often unresponsive organisations. There were few attempts to involve users or employees, and information disclosure was restricted.

Public sector trade union density was high but industrial democracy was weak and fragmented. Spending cuts in the late 1970s, imposed as a result of IMF intervention, drastically slowed down the building of new schools, hospitals, transport and community facilities.

Internal reform was a feasible alternative, but the Tories characteristically exploited service dissatisfaction to enforce privatisation. It is now common practice to portray nationalisation as a 'failure from any standpoint' and to describe services as 'inefficient'. But this exaggerated criticism fails to recognise that if they were so bad, how were they privatised so quickly, and why were investors so eager to acquire shares? The government spent millions preparing public assets for sale, but not on improving services.

Labour's Modernisation Agenda

The Labour government's objectives for public services and the welfare state have been cloaked in the rhetoric of the 'Third Way' and modernisation. Some of the objectives are hidden behind public statements proclaiming 'what matters is what works', and indisputably agreeable but vague statements about modernisation and renewal.

Blair's new vision for local government identified three reasons for change; locality's lack of a sense of direction, a lack of coherence in delivering local services, and wide variation in the quality of local services. But 'there is no future in the old model of councils trying to plan and run most services' (DETR, 1998a, p. 5, John Prescott in Foreword and Introduction). Instead local government is expected to create a Third Way in which local authorities will develop a vision for their locality, provide a focus for partnership and 'guarantee services for all' yet directly deliver only 'some services'.

A key difference is Labour's commitment to democratic renewal and innovation in council structures. However, democratic renewal is primarily about improving voter turnout and reinventing individual participation, since there is scant evidence of commitment and resources for community development, improving democratic accountability of user and community organisations. It is not designed to strengthen civil society, but rather to encourage the takeover of service delivery. The government is assuming that users will support them against the interests of the providers and the 'under-performing' or 'failing' local authorities. There is slightly less emphasis on the dogmatic drive towards private ownership and more emphasis on partnership with business and welfare state pluralism.

Labour's modernisation project is based on minimum reversal of Tory legislation. In practice, this has meant the continuation of Conservative style transformation although some policies are repackaged and justified by different objectives. The Labour government continued the commitment to:

- the transition to a performance-competition state in which, albeit voluntary, competitive tendering is legitimised across the public sector, not limited to defined services;
- a national programme of privatisation, although on a smaller scale;
- externalisation and transfer of local government (which is continuing at the same, if not faster, rate primarily because of Labour's belief in the enabling model) has been institutionalised in the Best Value regime;
- escalating corporatisation and commercialisation of the state, with increasing use of company structures;
- substantially increased role for private funding of the infra-structure and public services;
- a flexible labour market;
- a greater commitment to promote fairness and flexibility but making redistribution and equality matters of local choice.

The Conservative era had its three Es – efficiency, economy and effectiveness (but not equality, employment, equity, or environment). Labour promotes the four Cs – challenge, compare, consult and competitiveness – as a management process, but the same three Es form the statutory definition of Best Value! (Local Government Act 1999).

Promoting and Resisting Transformation

The Thatcher strategy was to establish new quasi-public organisations, such as Training and Enterprise Councils and NHS Trusts, which were then packed with government approved appointees. At the same time these organisations had terms of reference and budgets which gave them little scope other than to implement Tory policies.

Successive Conservative governments attempted to diminish the power of the professional classes whom they saw as a major block to their reform programme. The aim was to increase the power of managers, hence the emphasis on performance management and the establishment of a strong business role in decision-making. Not surprisingly, power struggles ensued between policy makers and managers and between managers and professional staff over the implementation of government policy.

6

The state is responsible for a wide range of interrelated services. It is extremely difficult to coordinate service delivery, develop integrated policies for a diverse range of interrelated issues, manage networks of organisations and meet changing demands with limited resources. It has to be innovative and creative yet carry out statutory duties with clockwork regularity. There is no perfect organisational or operational model, hence there will always be a point of conflict between political and economic interests.

A Theory of the Transformation Process

Although the transformation process may sometimes appear to be disjointed or uncoordinated, seven interrelated processes can be clearly identified:

Destabilisation: Unrelenting criticism of public services, often by generalising individual failures, while simultaneously ignoring achievements, or the cause of genuine problems and scale of social needs, is intended to undermine confidence in public provision. It portrays the public sector as inflexible and inefficient, problematic and having an inability to reform. Uncertainty, insecurity and doubts about the future role of public bodies sets in. It often involves the replacement of senior management and widespread use of management consultants. Severing the relationship between users and producers, between service quality and employment, together with an increased use of agency and casualised labour, all help to weaken staff, trade union and organisational resistance.

Disinvestment: Public spending cuts and new centralised financial controls result in continued under-investment in the infrastructure. Repairs, refurbishment and replacement needs are deliberately ignored or given low priority, simultaneously creating 'need' and demonstrating public sector 'inadequacy' in the minds of users, staff and the public.

Restructuring and commodification: Activities and functions are redefined, services repackaged, subsidiaries sold and activities curtailed. Service delivery is decentralised but strategic policy is centralised. Opting out and transfers lead to fracturing of services and organisations.

Marketisation and privatisation: Legislation is usually required to establish new funding arrangements. This imposes highly regulated competition within the state sector (in contrast to arm's-length regulation of privatised services), with regulatory frameworks for new markets and a more restricted role for public sector bodies in direct service provision. Services are packaged into contracts to meet the requirements of the market, not social and user needs.

New organisations and organisational restructuring: New organisations and structures are designed to accommodate the new policy agenda, in which unified services are divided into purchaser and provider functions, and to bridge the public–private divide. Organisational change reinforces management control to challenge traditional professional interests, particularly in health and education. Zones, projects and initiatives apply specific rules which are the gateway to public and private sector resources. These rules often include client/contractor or purchaser/provider structures and competitive tendering.

New managerial and operational systems: New operational rules, changed value systems and business involvement are moulded into 'modernisation' of the public sector to make it 'fit' to implement the new agenda.

New funding competitions: Regeneration resources have increasingly been allocated to local authorities via competitive bidding. Similarly, they must compete for private funding and approval of infrastructure projects.

The imposition of many of these policies was experimental and crude. Despite the political rhetoric, there was scant research evidence to show that they would be effective and there were few attempts to quantify their full public cost. There was also a blatant disregard for social and economic equity.

II
Role of the State

Economic Management

The management of the economy provided the framework for transformation. A new economic orthodoxy emerged in the 1980s based on controlling inflation primarily by interest rates, accompanied by a tight reign on public sector pay and total public spending. This meant encouraging the restructuring of the economy, in particular manufacturing industry. A prime aim was to cut income tax and reduce public sector borrowing. Productivity was to be improved through closures and downsizing. Thus, direct state intervention was reduced and the financial, regulatory and labour market conditions for business were created. Wide ranging deregulation included the removal of capital controls to allow the free flow of capital, and reform of trade unions and labour markets.

Social policy was dominated by the trickle-down theory and the emergence of a so-called property and share owning 'classless society'. The financial strategy has encompassed reducing state expenditure relative to GDP, selling public assets, transferring taxation from income to consumption, and at the same time centralising control of public spending and an internal drive to increase efficiency and better targeting of resources.

The 1997 Labour government continued the commitment to macroeconomic stability and the control of inflation. Labour adopted the Conservatives' public expenditure plans for the first two years of the administration and went further than the Tories in handing over responsibility for setting interest rates to the Bank of England.

Commodifying Services

Commodification describes the process of shaping and packaging services into saleable and marketable items, separating them from other activities, specifying their content and establishing a pricing structure. Their form and content is determined by market forces rather than public policy so that they can be traded, tendered and made the subject of a contract.

Services, property assets, products and public sector organisations and agencies have been subjected to commodification. The aim is to make public requirements and collective needs private and to seek to satisfy them individually. Community care is one example. The NHS and Community Care Act 1990 made local authorities primarily responsible for assessing need and coordinating care in the community in a context of increasing demand for home care services, budget cuts and legislation which encouraged the growth of private care. The home help service has been divided into 'personal care' and 'domestic assistance' activities. Families, neighbours and volunteers are encouraged to take over the household activities without compensation.

The public flotation of the utilities was another example. Unwanted subsidiary companies were sold, debts written off, assets valued cheaply, and free and discounted shares helped to ensure a price advantage, a marketable product and a 'successful' sale.

Commodification changes peoples expectations and values, particularly municipal or civic values. The climate of cuts has meant fewer resources, changing priorities to 'protect front-line services' such as education, and less public presence, such as staff in parks and public places.

Commodification provides new modes of accumulation for capital and new markets permit capital to profit from the provision of services previously provided by the state.

Services which were previously privately delivered are now being recommodified or repackaged to facilitate private delivery once again. The commodification process is limitless. Some services may appear to be rooted in the public sector today, both technically and politically; however, changes in demands and market forces could facilitate commodification later. Privately financed services enable capital to have a more direct role in the commodification of services. Private capital already effectively controls the supply of land, design and construction processes but now also influences the packaging and supply of finance, the operation of services and the use of surplus assets. Commodification becomes a permanent function of government with the state taking on the role of a 'privatisation or estate agency', a model adopted in many developing countries.

Education is being commodified by the separation of training, courses, and supplementary activities from core teaching, i.e. the segmentation of teaching into particular products which can be specified and thus delivered by other contractors, organisations or individuals. School buildings and their maintenance are separated from the core service provided within them, and core from non-core staff. Thus, schools are being established as individual entities, separate from the Local Education Authority (LEA) and collective educational planning. Individual school performance has become a key factor determining the school's 'attractiveness' and 'market position'.

The core/peripheral workforce model, increased use of temporary/casual staff and the use of self-employed/contract workers indicates that labour is also being commodified. Work, production and service schedules and staffing requirements are disaggregated with tasks allocated solely on the employer's minimal requirements.

Ideology and Language

The transformation process generates a new language and concepts. The *enabling* model of government, which is *provider neutral*, implies that there is no difference between public, private or voluntary provision. It also panders to the right's claim that in-house services are, by definition, provider led. It also marginalises employment and equalities policies. Local authorities and public bodies have *corporate* policies but the corporate sector usually means big business. There are terms which are increasingly ideologically confusing such as Clinton's *'market democracy'* and the British government's attempt to develop *'a culture of business-friendly enforcement'* through Local Business Partnerships under Labour's Better Regulation Initiative. The *'stakeholder economy'* and *'don't say no to business'* have significant implications. Internationally, phrases such as *'sustainable development'*, *'alleviating or eradicating poverty'*, *'ecological and environmental sustainability'* and *'development finance'* are widely used with the assumption that policies and investment automatically produce 'development', reduce poverty and improve the environment.

We have to be very clear about terms and definitions to prevent evasion and deception. A 'non-tiered National Health Service free at the point of use' could mean a privately operated NHS but still providing free care. Similarly, 'a solid state pension as the first building block in the pension system' could mean that the state pension is publicly funded but operated by private firms and/or has a declining role as part of a privately dominated three-pillar pension structure. The advocates of stakeholding usually avoid any reference to publicly funded and provided services. So language does matter. Language is an important tool to facilitate changes in the principles or to erode the value of universality, solidarity and redistribution and to move from collective provision to individual responsibility. A new language has emerged – risk transfer, bankability, business case – to justify partnership and private finance projects in the public sector. Labour's emphasis on 'what matters is what works' places priority on achieving success first, with the means being of secondary importance. Procurement, commissioning and brokerage are now part of the Third Way language.

Privatisation and Transfer

The Conservatives often justified privatisation in terms of 'rolling back the frontiers of the state' but this is a false description masking increased central control and the redirection of resources to business. While the sale of state-owned corporations, land and property has been the financial driving force, different forms of privatisation support other aspects of transformation of the state, for example competitive tendering and state subsidies for private services. The state has always bought and sold property, purchased services and encouraged enterprise, but the scale of privatisation in the past two decades has been unparalleled.

If one thing has been consistent over the past two decades, it is the relentless rolling process of privatisation. What is unthinkable to privatise today becomes feasible tomorrow and a reality shortly thereafter. A political economy typology identifies eight forms of privatisation and deregulation:

● private ownership
● private production of public services
● private finance
● transfer of services
● increased domestic/family responsibility
● deregulation, liberalisation and re-regulation
● expansion of private services
● commercialisation of public services.

The rapid rationalisation and restructuring of nationalised industries and manufacturing industries in the early 1980s included closures of pits, shipyards, steel plants, hospitals and factories, contributing to mass unemployment and the decline of communities and regions. Direct state intervention in industrial sectors and/or firms was curtailed as resources were targeted internally to financially and politically sustain the privatisation and marketisation programme. The Thatcher government instead focused on share giveaways, debt write-offs, tax concessions and fees to financiers rather than investment in the areas ravaged by decline and closures. Economic management centred on reducing inflation with no commitment to maintain high and stable levels of employment. Wage restraint, labour market reform and reduced corporate taxation were considered essential to create more productive and profitable economic conditions and inward investment.

Alleged efficiency improvement has been one of the main claims made to justify privatisation. Privatisation originated as a political and financial strategy and the economic rationale was appended later after the Tories had won a second general election in 1983. It has become institutionalised under the centre-right political consensus of the three main political parties, although differences remain over which services could be privatised. The rationale for privatisation changed from its initial focus on the state withdrawing from ownership of the utilities and nationalised industries to one which is not dependent on the state directly operating services or owning the facilities in which they are provided.

Gas, water, electricity, telecommunications and state owned companies such as British Airways, British Aerospace and Associated British Ports were sold through stock market flotations with emphasis placed on 'people's capitalism' to widen share ownership. The privatisation programme also encouraged land and property sales, particularly council houses of which 2.2 million were sold between 1979 and 1999. These sales were accompanied by 100 local authority full or partial stock transfers (over 400,000 dwellings) to housing associations. Almost 5,000 school playing fields were sold for development in the last ten years of the Conservative government. Gross privatisation receipts in the period 1979–99 were nearly £125 billion with the utilities and energy sector accounting for £25 billion, telecommunications £16 billion, with land and property sales accounting for half the total.

The 1990s privatisation programme completed the sale of most of the remaining nationalised industries and shifted the emphasis to the sale and transfer of local authority services, franchising the rail network and imposing competition in all public bodies. Other forms of privatisation included the payment of residential care allowances to the elderly in private residential care homes, which increased from £11 million in 1977–8 to £2.6 billion by 1993 and led to the rapid growth of a state-financed private care sector. The private pensions industry grew rapidly after the government allowed opting out of the State Earnings-Related Pension Scheme with concessions on national insurance. Student tuition fees and training and nursery vouchers were examples of other forms of privatisation.

Labour has replaced the Conservative overt objectives with pragmatism and partnership, with a less strident ideological commitment but with an equally widespread creation of opportunities for private accumulation. Following the publication of the National Asset Register in 1997, Labour has continued with a national privatisation programme with £4 billion annual receipts planned between 1998 and 2001. Planned sales include the National Air Traffic Services, a further tranche of student loans, Belfast Port, the Commonwealth Development Corporation and the Royal Mint.

Externalisation of Public Resources

By 2000, over 100 local authorities had externalised Direct Service Organisations, technical services, financial and information technology services, transferred leisure, arts and residential care to trusts and/or transferred all or part of their housing stock to housing associations. The privatisation of 15 Next Steps Agencies brought the total number of externalised services to 327 which involved the transfer of 68,150 staff to private firms or to non-profit organisations. Externalisation is primarily motivated by financial savings and access to private capital for repairs and improvements. Although European law affords transferred staff a degree of protection, it does not apply to new staff and most private contractors have inferior terms and conditions. It enables the employer to restructure with more flexible working patterns.

Outsourcing contracts has increased under Labour with many multi-service contracts transferring 500 or more staff. The annual council housing transfer programme has been increased from 30,000 to 140,000 per annum and the floodgates could open as several major cities, such as Glasgow and Birmingham, plan total stock transfers. Transfer receipts, net of debt repayment and other costs, increased from £44 million in 1996–7 (the last year of Conservative government) to £116 million in 1998–9 after two years of the Labour administration. If transfers rise to 300,000 homes per annum, council housing will cease to exist within a decade.

Education is another service where marketisation and privatisation is creating a 'new education economy'. The role of Local Education Authorities (LEAs) has come in for savage criticism from the government and the Office for Standards in Education (OFSTED) spearheaded by Chris Woodhead. Education authorities are responsible for strategic management of the education service including planning and allocating resources, access (school places and transport), support for school improvement, special education services and offering services to schools. Whilst many LEAs have been slow to innovate and improve services (paying 'lip service' to school autonomy with a 'nostalgia for control' according to OFSTED) the response to this problem is familiar: don't fix it, privatise it, centralise it, threaten abolition and justify it with management consultants.

Of 44 LEA inspections by OFSTED in 1999, some 40 per cent of authorities were claimed to have 'significant weaknesses'. Inspections in other authorities in 2000 increased the list of 'failing LEAs'. The government responded by:

- Using powers to intervene in authorities by directing them to outsource and privatise education services.
- Inviting management consultants and education service contractors to carry out these interventions.
- Supporting a pilot procurement 'brokerage' scheme in Rotherham, devised by management consultants Office of Public Management, which will enable schools to purchase services such as payroll, information technology, management and curriculum support, school meals and cleaning directly from private firms.
- Channelling additional investment to schools directly from central government and threatening to bypass local authorities by separating school funding and LEA funding as part of its 'frontline first' initiative.

These government initiatives, together with business involvement in Education Action Zones and Public / Private Partnership (PPP) schemes for school buildings and private management of 'failing schools', like those in Hackney, Islington and Leeds, signal the rapid expansion of the education market. The business of education is booming, with 30 takeovers worth £1 billion in a 16 month period between 1999–2000. Britain is providing a model for the World Bank's EdInvest service which facilitates private investment in education in developing countries and the global education market.

'Strategic partnership' is the new mantra under which local authorities outsource a large array of services. Access to private capital and/or information technology are a minor part of the rationale for 'strategic partnership'. The driving force is primarily 'the modernisation agenda' and the belief that partnerships with private companies are, *per se,* the only way forward. The feast of large multi-million pound long term contracts under Labour makes the Tories Compulsory Competitive Tendering regime look like a roadside picnic.

The implications of 'strategic partnerships' are more far reaching than PPPs, because under the guise of partnership, markets, competition and procurement are embedded into core public services in the heart of local government, placing companies in a powerful position and able to manoeuvre for additional services.

Personalising Social Need
Diluting people's expectations of government so as to encourage greater reliance on market, family or individual provision was a key Conservative objective. The state has been an ideological battleground in terms of public versus private ownership and in-house provision versus private contractors. The concept of the 'enabling state' has been at the heart of this ideological confrontation, a model of government in which the state facilitates and supports but services are primarily provided through the private and social economy. Three key trends have emerged: individualising, localising and neutralising service delivery.

'Consumer sovereignty' is promoted as an individual right, not a collective one. The Citizen's Charter and the promotion of customer care with service standards and complaints procedures has resulted in service users being treated as individual purchasers of services, confining the relationship to the point of service delivery or consumption. The end, not the means, is what counts, governments have claimed. The interface between service delivery and the user is thus depoliticised. Need and class are deliberately ignored as consumers are treated as a homogeneous group of individuals with little or no collective identity. The user is encouraged to think only of how the service relates to them personally. The creation of 'one-stop-shops' and call centres are a service improvement but equally a further manifestation of individual consumption. Government is seeking to privatise operational failures to prevent them becoming public issues around which people might organise and campaign.

'Opting out' of publicly provided services, such as education and health, fragments and destabilises public services and encourages a narrower, more localised and more self-interested concern. It is a consumerist version of democracy and democratic rights. With the individualisation of identity, concern and action becomes more and more focused on the home, reinforced by 'family values'.

III
Financing the State

Restructuring Public Finance

Globalisation and neo-liberalism have created pressures to radically reform taxation which has led to the redistribution of taxation and to demands for reducing public spending. Reagan cut US business rates from 46 to 34 per cent in 1986, corporation tax in Britain was systematically reduced from 52 to 30 per cent between 1982 and 1999 and Germany reduced corporate taxation from 37 to 25 per cent between 1980 and 1994. The redirection of taxation is demonstrated by Canada where individuals contributed 29 per cent of taxation income compared with the corporate sector's 18 per cent in 1966 but by 1996 the individual/corporate ratio was 43/10. Companies and the self-employed contributed 13.1 per cent of Germany's tax burden in 1983 but these had more than halved to 5.7 per cent by 1995.

State Expenditure

A combination of financial controls, cuts in public spending and the proceeds of privatisation helped the Conservative government to partly achieve its objective of reducing government spending as a proportion of national income. It was 42 per cent in 1979–80, rose during the recession in the early 1980s, hovered at 38–39 per cent until the early 1990s when it rose to 43 per cent, only to decline to 39 per cent in 1998–9. Privatisation proceeds reached a high of £8.2 billion in 1992–3, totalling some £71 billion (1995–6 prices) in the 1979–98 period. These proceeds helped to keep the Public Sector Borrowing Requirement lower than it would otherwise have been and, combined with a transfer of taxation from incomes to consumer expenditure, provided the means for cuts in personal income and corporate taxation.

New Control Mechanisms

Increased centralisation of spending controls has been a key feature of government in the past two decades. The switch to the disastrous poll tax, later replaced by the council tax, together with the nationalisation of business rates (property tax) has reduced the scope for local financial decision-making. Central government determines each local authority's expenditure through a Standard Spending Assessment coupled with a financial clawback if the authority 'overspends'. Additional regulations limit the income local authorities can generate. Strict control of allowances for additional statutory responsibilities, inflation and pay awards enforce budget cuts and hence 'efficiency savings'.

Quangos have generally been centrally financed and a number of Funding Councils were set up to allocate public money to the education sector. Quango budgets were, in effect, ringfenced and the new organisations were able to retain surpluses and build up reserves of public money outside of democratic control. For example, the 74 Training and Enterprise Councils in England held over £285 million in accumulated reserves at 31 March 1997, a 10 per cent increase on the previous year. Many schools under local management have accumulated reserves although they often bear little relation to educational needs.

The use of the National Lottery for funding arts and culture, sports and leisure facilities, community and 'non-core' health and educational activities has in effect nationalised and privatised the finance of these activities. The award of lottery grants lacks democratic accountability and is another example of transferring taxation from income to consumption.

Changing Boundaries Between Public/Private Welfare

There have been significant changes in the financing of public/private services since 1979. The proportion of publicly provided services has declined from 60.8 per cent in 1979–80 to 51.4 per cent in 1995–6, a decline of over 15 per cent. The proportion of different forms of privately financed services increased from 27.8 per cent to 31.4 per cent in the same period.

Different Forms of Private Finance

User charges: NHS prescription charges soared from 20p in 1979 to £6.00 by 2000 although 80 per cent of prescriptions are dispensed to exempt groups such as children, the elderly and claimants. Dental charges have also increased steeply with non-exempt patients paying 80 per cent of the cost of NHS dental check-ups and treatment. Funding for sight tests was withdrawn in 1989 and these are now carried out privately at an average cost of £13.20. Most local authorities have introduced charges for home care services. Student loans were introduced in 1990 and the means tested maintenance grant for living expenses was abolished in 1999, forcing more and more students to work part-time. Not surprisingly, the number of over-21s applying for degree courses declined by 11 per cent in 1998, as did the proportion of applicants from unskilled and skilled manual households.

Private use of public facilities: The NHS has over 3,000 pay beds and is the single largest supplier of private health care in Britain. Revenue from private patients increased in the 1970s and soared by 230 per cent between 1979/80 and 1995/6.

Withdrawal of services: NHS eye frames were restricted to children, low income and special needs in 1985 and shortly thereafter replaced by vouchers. NHS dentists are increasingly difficult to locate as an increasing proportion of dentists attend only private patients.

Subsidies and rebates: Opting out of SERPS was encouraged from 1986 with over 5 million people receiving rebates on National Insurance contributions for personal pensions.

Tax relief: Tax relief on private medical insurance contracts for individuals aged 60 or over increased from £40 million in 1990–1 to £110 million in 1996–7, yet the number of contracts only increased 20 per cent to 600,000 in the same period.

Discounts: Council tenants had up to 50 per cent discounts for the purchase of their homes under the Right to Buy legislation which totalled £24.2 billion in the 1979/80–1996/7 period.

Internal Drive to Increase Efficiency and Better Targeting of Resources

The control and allocation of public expenditure, particularly to local government, has been a very important means of enforcing the transformation of the state. Public spending cuts have been used to impose a political discipline on public bodies as much as for their economic function. Management by objectives and accountable management were basic themes following the Fulton Report in 1968. The Financial Management Initiative was launched in central government in 1982 and included setting objectives and management by results, the delegation of budgets, the creation of cost centres to establish management accountability together with better management accounting systems and training. The Audit Commission, formed in 1983, strove to apply the 3Es (efficiency, economy and effectiveness) in local government, and later in the NHS, although efficiency and cost dominated the agenda.

The focus on the distribution of the cake has prevented debate on the appropriate size of the cake and the required level of taxation. Increased expenditure has been limited to additional income as a result of higher than expected growth in the economy, and further internal efficiency savings or raids on the contingency reserve.

Competitive bidding within a centralised system has increasingly been used in the 1990s to allocate resources for regeneration (City Challenge and the Single Regeneration Budget), housing and local capital investment. Bidding represents a retreat from matching scarce resources to social need and is a means of enforcing central government policy objectives on local government. It provides only limited new investment because it masks cuts in mainline programmes and incurs a high financial, institutional and opportunity cost in bidding.

Accountancy Changes

The 1990 NHS reforms also introduced resource or accrual accounting, following its adoption in Australia and New Zealand. It is being introduced through central and local government in 2001. In theory, accrual output-based budgeting is a process through which public bodies are funded and monitored on the basis of performance outputs and full costs and liabilities. The claimed advantages are that it is customer focused, based on the supply of services/products, and separates purchaser and provider. This supposedly reflects full accrual costs, gives clear choices to the buyer, provides a sound basis for internal resource allocation and focuses on outputs and outcomes. However, there has been extensive criticism that a commercial accountancy system is not applicable to the public sector.

Partnerships and Private Finance

Infrastructure investment in Britain declined dramatically after the 1973 oil crisis and International Monetary Fund intervention three years later. Both Labour and Conservative governments imposed substantive cuts in public sector capital spending programmes. Net public sector investment under the Labour government, (£29.9 billion, 5.8 per cent of GDP) in 1974–5, more than halved by the end of the decade and plummeted to a mere 0.4 per cent of GDP in 1988–9, increasing in the early 1990s, to decline again to only 0.6 per cent of GDP for the first three years of the 1997 Labour government. The decline in public sector investment in the last two decades occurred at the same time as the government had unprecedented privatisation receipts and North Sea Oil revenues and public money which has been squandered on tax cuts for business and the wealthy.

'Taxpayers no longer need to own hospital buildings' claimed the Treasury (Private Finance Panel, 1996, p. 7). The Labour government embraced Public / Private Partnerships with fervour: 'Privatisation was their solution. Modernisation is ours. PPPs are central to that modernisation process ...' stated Alan Milburn, Secretary of State for Health in 1999. Labour's commitment is rooted in four claims:

● The government is using private capital as an addition to public investment 'to close the all-too-clear gap that exists between the quality of our public sector buildings and facilities and those of the private sector'.

● The public sector needs the commercial expertise to help manage the complex investment processes in IT, transport and other services.

● PPPs result in better services and better value for money, i.e. efficiency savings.

● The switch to focus on outcomes, not inputs, means that the risks of delivering outputs are transferred to the private sector.

The case for Private Finance Initiatives (PFI) and Public Private Partnerships (PPP) has shifted from a financial justification to one where the value for money argument is paramount, coupled with the belief that the private sector is superior to the public sector in terms of management, expertise, efficiency and quality. Both the National Audit Office report (NAO, 1999) and the Andersen report for the Treasury Taskforce (Arthur Andersen, 2000) made unsubstantiated claims of 10–20 per cent efficiency savings. Although the Treasury continues its fiscal stringency to ensure that PFI is the prime way to finance capital schemes, PPP/PFI projects are considered an essential part of the public services modernising agenda.

By 1997 a large part of the transport, energy and utilities and communications infrastructure was owned and operated by the private sector. It left the social and welfare state, defence and criminal justice system infrastructure in the public sector which subsequently became prime targets for privatisation.

There are various types of PPP but the most common in Britain requires the private sector to design, build, finance and operate (DBFO) facilities, usually for 25–35 years (7–15 years for equipment). It finances construction and is repaid by the state, in regular payments for the use of the buildings and for the services provided under a facilities management contract. Payments are classified as revenue, not capital and thus do not count against public borrowing and do not commence until the building is completed. It thus has enormous short-term political appeal.

What Labour did for PPPs
The new Labour government acted quickly in 1997, setting up and implementing the Bates Review which recommended streamlining the PFI process. The government also rushed through legislation to clarify the powers of NHS Trusts and local authorities to enter into PFI agreements and guarantee financial payments over the life of the contract irrespective of public expenditure. In other words, PFI contract payments are ring-fenced. They also established new

processing and prioritising procedures for PPP projects in all government departments. They also removed the requirement that all public sector capital projects be tested for private finance potential. This ensured that only 'bankable' projects were prioritised. PFI was heavily promoted in local government which had lagged well behind other sectors. The Labour government appears to have a better understanding of the needs of business than the right-wing ideologues of the previous administration!

Net public infrastructure investment is planned to increase to £19 billion per annum by 2003/4, representing 1.8 per cent of GDP. However, a further £21 billion of PFI deals are expected to be signed in the same period. By late 2000, nearly 350 PFI projects had been signed with a capital value of £25 billion. A further 227 projects were at an advanced stage. The welfare state infrastructure accounted for 19 per cent of the value of projects. However, this is a misleading indicator of the scale of PFI projects because it excludes projects which have been centrally approved but not signed and those which have been advertised following a local decision to proceed. The combined value of these last two categories far exceeds the value of signed projects.

Private finance is presented as an alternative form of procurement by converting the payment of debt incurred in obtaining assets into revenue payments as a payment for services. This is reflected in the presentation of the capital value of PFI projects. For example, a London Borough of Haringey secondary schools project has an £87 million capital project but the total PFI payment is £233 million over 25 years. Similarly, the South Buckinghamshire NHS Trust's £45 million new hospital will in fact require a total payment of £244.7 million to United Healthcare over 30 years.

Transformation of the funding of capital expenditure: Local authority PFI schemes receive the same subsidy as public sector capital schemes via the Revenue Support Grant, controlled by central government PFI credits for approved projects. PFI credits have soared from £250 million in 1997–8 to £1,600 million in 2003/4. Since the 1990 Health Service reforms, capital spending has been financed internally by NHS trusts having to make an annual surplus of income over expenditure equal to 6 per cent of the value of their assets (buildings and equipment) and to make a charge for depreciation through capital charges. Capital spending is heavily dependent on NHS trusts including capital charges in prices charged to purchasers, receipts from property and land sales, and NHS trust efficiency savings.

PFI consortia are refinancing deals to substantially increase profits. For example, Group 4 and construction group Carillion almost doubled their returns from the Fazakerley (now Altcourse) prison contract. Profits increased by £14.1 million (75 per cent since 1995) of which £10.7 million came from refinancing (extending the bank loan period at a reduced interest rate and early repayment of other debt), £3.4 million from completing the prison ahead of schedule and lower construction costs. The Prison Service received £1 million for additional termination liabilities.

In early 2000, Morrison Construction packaged five PFI projects in a joint venture with Edison Capital, a financial services subsidiary of the US electricity company Edison International. It is the first example of bundling PFI projects and a step towards the creation of a secondary market.

Refinancing and a secondary market of PPP/PFI projects are likely to have an increasing impact on the scope and content of PPPs generally. The PPP lobby consistently under-estimates or deliberately ignores the power that international financial capital and market forces will ultimately have in determining the provision of public services. Yet marketisation means precisely that market forces are bound to have a powerful influence in the division of labour, risk allocation and the provision of core services.

Spiral of Decline and Opportunity

Cuts in public sector capital spending create a downward spiral of decline starting with reduced maintenance, postponed improvements, physical deterioration of the infrastructure, rising user complaints and pressure to use alternative sources of funding. But this process also creates a spiral of opportunity for business.

Changing relationship between capital and the state: PPPs represent capital and the state forging a new relationship based on negotiated deals, long-term service contracts, shared risk and guaranteed payments irrespective of the state of public finances. Compulsory Competition Tendering (CCT) and market testing were almost entirely labour-only contracts, but PPPs require the private sector to provide capital assets, as well as maintenance and a wide range of support services. Capital is further embedded in the planning and delivery of public services and extends the enabling model of government.

Transforming the procurement process: PPP imposes a new and more complex procurement process in the public sector. The PPP process is part tendering (to select a preferred bidder) and part contract negotiation in which public bodies and PPP consortia and their advisers haggle behind closed doors. It requires public bodies to develop comprehensive project appraisal and evaluation methodologies and the ability to monitor large performance contracts to ensure contract payments are performance related and that risk is fairly attributed in practice. The criteria used by the Treasury's Project Review Group, the National Audit Office and the Public Sector Comparator (merely an investment appraisal) ignore equality, employment and environmental sustainability and socioeconomic factors. Hence they do not take into account the deeper and wider implications of PPP projects.

PPPs extend marketisation of services far deeper and wider than competitive tendering ever could. It virtually eliminates in-house competition (on grounds that there is no transfer of risk if services remain in-house) and smaller companies (because of large long-term contracts and equity capital in the consortia). Transaction costs are high, up to four times those of competitive tendering, but from the multinationals' perspective they form a useful barrier to market entry, and are ultimately funded by the public sector.

New form of contractor organisation: PPPs require the formation of a 'special purpose vehicle' or operating company, a separate company in which the construction contractor, financial institutions and facilities management contractor have an equity stake. This company manages and operates the facility including selling spare capacity and vacant space to third parties. The combining of finance, construction and support service companies into a new owner-operator industry has been warmly welcomed by the Confederation of British Industry.

Reconfiguring services: The government emphasises that PPPs are contracts for services, not buildings, which makes the distinction between support services such as building maintenance, cleaning, catering, transport and other related services, and core services such as teaching and medical treatment, divisive and unsustainable in the longer term. State withdrawal from ownership and management of the infrastructure has profound implications for core services. PPP consortia will eventually include private companies bidding to manage schools and local education authorities or private health care companies.

The commodification of service provision results in social needs being subordinate to financial flows stemming from usage or activity levels, user charges and income generation. The distinctiveness of the public sector is eroded to ease transferability between public and private sectors and the former is reshaped into a residual role.

Changes in construction industry: PPPs have accelerated construction industry expansion into facilities management, extending the scope of the industry from design, construction, and building maintenance to a wide range of support services.

Further centralisation: The government claims that PPPs are 'services' contracts, normally for local decision-making, but the Treasury ultimately controls approvals through the Projects Review Group. This is another example of the centralisation of decision-making which will be more extensive in 2020 if PPPs continue at their current rate.

Changing nature of risk: The public sector has always borne the risk of facilities requiring adaptation as service needs change, of re-letting or changing the use of buildings. Long-terms deals are currently being signed on a static concept of risk transfer. But the nature of risk will change as the private sector gains increasing control of the infrastructure and delivery of support services. It will then be able to strongly influence, if not control, the supply chains of users, the growth of private services in 'public' facilities and third party use of spare capacity. Risk is identified, quantified, attributed and priced; in other words it is monetised.

Privatising the development process: Gaining control of surplus land and buildings such as school playing fields, vacant land, empty hospital buildings, and so on, for property development is a key part of PPP projects for the private sector. They often provide a key source of finance and profit and ensure that surplus public assets are sold for private development.

Transformation of the labour process: The government and PFI consortia claim that the higher cost of privately financed projects will be more than offset by the private sector's 'better utilisation of assets' and increased operational savings. Facilities management contracts are intended to integrate services which have often been separately tendered. Increased productivity and financial savings from support services are a core requirement for the viability of most PPPs.

Reversing policy: If PFI spending was replaced by conventional forms of public funding, the selling of an extra £3–4 billion of gilts annually in current circumstances would seem to pose no problems. Abolition of PPP/PFI would not affect the Treasury's current fiscal rules – the golden rule that on average over the economic cycle the government will borrow only to invest and not to fund revenue expenditure and the sustainable investment rule that public sector net debt as a proportion of GDP will be held at a stable and prudent level. Nor would abolition affect the Maastricht convergence criteria, established for countries wishing to join the European Monetary Union, which limit government borrowing (to 3 per cent of GDP) and government debt (to 60 per cent of GDP).

If the Government adopted the General Government Financial Deficit for public sector current and capital expenditure accounting, replacing the Public Sector Net Borrowing (PSNB which replaced the Public Sector Borrowing Requirement), public bodies could borrow to invest from the European Investment Bank (EIB) and the European Investment Fund (EIF) at low rates of interest. Following the Amsterdam Treaty in 1997, both the EIB and EIF directly fund schemes under the Special Action Programme for investment in health, education, housing, regeneration and environmental projects. Since their funds are not guaranteed by governments, they do not count against public borrowing except in Britain and the Netherlands. The PSNB is in surplus and rather than paying off national debt, the government should be investing in the infrastructure.

IV
Undermining Local Democracy

Company status has been used extensively in the last 20 years to separate activities and functions from public bodies and from direct democratic control. Companies have separate legal status and are controlled by directors with strict financial and operational obligations under the Companies Acts. Company status therefore separates, divides and ring-fences activities and services into a stand-alone economic entity with a separate decision-making structure, budget, accounts and responsibilities. They survive according to their balance sheet, increased productivity and diversification and, not surprisingly, are forced to adopt commercial values and practices. Most public sector companies do not have to pay dividends to shareholders but must make a surplus to finance investment.

Many public bodies formed companies for commercial income-generating activities or for specific activities such as economic development and regeneration. Local authorities were required to turn waste disposal operations into arm's-length commercial organisations following the Environmental Protection Act 1990. Municipal bus companies were operated on this basis before the Conservative government enforced their sale following the 1985 Transport Act. Polytechnics, now universities, and Further Education Colleges were transferred from local authority control to independent companies in the 1980s.

An increasing proportion of local services are now delivered and controlled by private or public sector companies.

Non-elected public bodies or non-governmental organisations have grown rapidly in the last decade. There were 6,424 quangos in 1996 (excluding government agencies) spending £60.4 billion annually which represented nearly 20 per cent of total government expenditure in 1994–5. There are three types of quangos. The majority are executive, implementing government policy and providing services in health, education, housing and training. Of the 5,750 executive quangos, 266 operate nationally, 318 at regional level and the remainder at local level. Regulatory quangos are mainly national bodies such as those established to supervise the privatised utilities. The third type, advisory quangos, are responsible for scientific, arts and specialist issues, for example, the Royal Fine Art Commission.

In addition to devolution in Scotland and Wales, the Labour government established nine new Regional Development Agencies (RDAs) in England, responsible for regional economic strategies bringing together inward investment, small firms, skills and training and regional development work. Their broad remit also includes administration of the Single Regeneration Budget Challenge Fund, the regeneration roles of English Partnerships and the Rural Development Commission, integrating transport planning, promoting public–private partnerships and technology transfer. Government appointed RDA boards are business-led with representation from local authorities, higher education and trade unions.

Public sector companies, trusts and boards have several common elements. The directors normally comprise local elites and business people. Elected Members and service users have minority representation or none at all. Democratic accountability is limited yet they are all dependent on public money for the bulk of their income. Staff and trade unions have limited or no representation. Subsidiary companies carry out commercial activities (usually dominated by business and managerial appointments) or specific functions (as a vehicle to give tenants greater participation).

Not surprisingly, increasing commercialisation of public services has led to the erosion of a public service ethos. A study of over 300 staff in four local authorities identified a shift in interpretations of accountability towards contract and market accountability and increasing dissatisfaction with rules which acted as obstacles to the effective and efficient management of their 'businesses'. It also found that fragmentation of local government into business units encouraged an inward-looking culture 'that requires individuals to place the interests of their own part of the organisation above those of any wider organisational, or societal, objectives'. Loyalties were moving away from a council-wide focus to cost centres and business units. 'The key feature about the emerging ethos of local government service is that it emphasises a competitive, contractual, insular and adversarial culture'.

The transfer of government functions to quasi-public bodies is, in effect, the privatisation of power. Public policy and investment decisions are made behind closed doors. Installing token democratic representation does little to change power relationships which are usually bound by 'commercial confidentiality' and restrictions on contact with the media. This represents both institutional and operational privatisation of government. These bodies increasingly operate a form of 'government by contract' in which contractual relationships determine service delivery, forms of accountability and relationships with other public bodies. Most of these organisations are run by people who are unelected, unaccountable to, and unrepresentative of, their local communities.

In its first year of power, the Labour government established nearly 200 policy reviews, task forces and advisory groups. While information about, and accountability of, some of the high profile reviews has been established, there is little knowledge of the terms of reference, membership, accountability, consultation procedures and reporting timetable available for the bulk of reviews. An analysis of the membership of 30 leading task forces and advisory groups revealed that 72 per cent were men, 29 per cent were from business and 6 per cent from trade unions. Only 13 out of 449 members (0.29 per cent) were black or Asian.

The Key Requirements of Best Value

Best Value is Labour's alternative to Compulsory Competitive Tendering and comparable with the Better Quality Services initiative in central government, which is described as a means of 'creating public/private partnerships through market testing and contracting out' (Cabinet Office, 1998b, cover). All government departments have Public Service Agreements which set out objectives, performance and efficiency targets. The NHS has a Performance Assessment Framework. Best Value is, in fact, a new control mechanism, albeit with the potential for local innovation. It is driven by performance measurement and auditing with the threat of government intervention if local authorities do not achieve continuous improvement.

Two general duties, to achieve Best Value and to consult widely, came into effect from April 2000. Authorities have to review approximately 20 per cent of their services annually so that all services are reviewed on a five-year cycle. Authorities are required to justify why and how a service is provided, to compare their performance with others using national and local indicators, to consult and engage with their local communities in reviewing services and to demonstrate competitiveness through rigorous comparison and competition. Compulsory tendering has been abolished but authorities are required to 'develop markets' by researching suppliers, engaging with potential suppliers and encouraging markets by 'packaging work appropriate to the market' (DETR, 1999, p. 14).

The government has repealed Part II of the Local Government Act 1988 to allow authorities to take into account terms and conditions of employment, equal opportunities policies, training and contracting out costs in the award of contracts. Local authorities are also subjected to a new duty to promote the economic, social and environmental well-being of the area, a duty to produce a community plan 'to secure the development of a comprehensive strategy for promoting the well-being of their area', and have new powers to enter into partnerships with public, private and voluntary organisations.

There are opportunities under the Best Value regime for local authorities to be innovative and creative, to add their own definition to the basic requirements and to improve the co-ordination and integration of services and activities. They can develop genuine user/employee involvement, new methods for service review and performance assessment, minimising competitive tendering and using Best Value to make the case for more resources.

Best Value is, however, also a substantial threat to staff and users because some councils are pressing ahead with an externalisation agenda, led by chief executives eager to impress as performance managers and enablers – the managerial careerist equivalent of the privatisation fat cats. Best Value could result in far more extensive competitive tendering than that achieved by the Conservative government because Best Value applies to all services rather than defined activities. Continued budget constraints could make 'more for less' a very negative experience for staff with increasing generic working, deskilling and changes to working practices and erosion of terms and conditions. Financial issues and efficiency measures are likely to dominate performance measurement leading to further marginalisation of equalities, health and safety and social justice issues.

Best Value will institutionalise comparisons with the private sector in terms of performance and cost. It focuses on quantifiable measures or 'public services by numbers'. Best Value seeks continue consumer consultation rather than user and employee involvement and will further marginalise social justice and equal opportunities. After two decades of the commercialisation of public service management, central and local government urgently need a framework which positively promotes public service management.

Conclusion

There is an urgent need to develop a new public order centred on the public delivery of public goods. It must be rooted in public ownership and control and in-house service provision which re-emphasises the importance of how and by whom services are delivered. Labour's 'What matters is what works' mantra must be terminated forthwith. It does matter who delivers services because the quality of jobs (skills, security, pay, pensions, health and safety) has a direct bearing on the quality of service. And the way in which public services are delivered is an integral part of their quality. Simply measuring performance at the point of use is fundamentally flawed.

We urgently need an alternative modernisation strategy. It must be constructed around:

- increased public investment and new financing mechanisms coupled with the abolition of the Private Finance Initiative;
- revitalisation of public services in place of transfers and privatisation;
- a new public service management with social justice auditing and planning to mainstream equity and equalities;
- genuine democratic accountability and user/employee involvement in policy-making, planning and management;
- more stringent regulation of markets and firms;
- rebuilding state capacity to strengthen its ability to intervene in the economy and to fulfil its core functions.

A new international financial and regulatory framework is also essential together with the termination of the World Trade Organisation's General Agreement on Trade in Services agenda which will only further embed Labour's brand of modernisation.

This pamphlet is reproduced from Dexter Whitfield's book Public Services or Corporate Welfare, *by kind permission of Pluto Press.*